Green **Line 3**

Vokabellernheft

Ernst Klett Verlag
Stuttgart • Leipzig

Vorwort

Dieses Vokabellernheft im Taschenformat enthält alle Wörter und Wendungen aus *Green Line* 3. Du kannst es überall hin mitnehmen, um Vokabeln zu lernen und zu wiederholen.
Am besten hast du beim Lernen immer einen Bleistift zur Hand. Damit markierst du Wörter und Wendungen, die dir besondere Schwierigkeiten bereiten. Diese kannst du dann in regelmäßigen Abständen immer wieder durchgehen.
Am Ende des Unit-Wortschatzes findest du zahlreiche Übungen, mit denen du das Gelernte ordnen und wiederholen kannst. Die Übungen helfen dir auch bei der Vorbereitung auf Vokabeltests.
Ab Seite 69 kannst du dann noch einige Puzzles lösen und, gemeinsam mit einem Partner / einer Partnerin, *Games* spielen. Ganz am Ende des Vokabellernhefts (S. 77–80) findest du die Liste der unregelmäßigen Verben.

Viel Spaß wünscht dir dein *Green Line*-Team!

LERNTIPP

Dein Gehirn arbeitet am besten, wenn du gut „drauf" bist. Bringe dich vor dem Lernen neuer Vokabeln in die richtige Stimmung. Höre deinen Lieblingssong, mache ein paar Kniebeugen, verschicke zum Beispiel eine nette SMS.

Unit 1 The world of sport

Check-in

oval ['əʊvl]	oval, eiförmig
pitch [pɪtʃ]	Spielfeld, Platz
referee [ˌrefr'i:]	Schiedsrichter / -in
to **control** [kən'trəʊl]	kontrollieren; steuern
baseball ['beɪsbɔ:l]	Baseball
ice [aɪs]	Eis
stick [stɪk]	Stock, Schläger
base [beɪs]	Base *(beim Baseball)*
field [fi:ld]	(Spiel)feld
bat [bæt]	Schläger *(beim Tischtennis, Baseball)*
cricket ['krɪkɪt]	Kricket
to **go on** [gəʊ‿'ɒn]	(an)dauern
athletics [æθ'letɪks]	Leichtathletik
rugby ['rʌgbi]	Rugby
track [træk]	Bahn, Laufbahn; Weg
skateboarding ['skeɪtbɔ:dɪŋ]	Skateboardfahren
American [ə'merɪkən]	Amerikanisch; amerikanisch, aus Amerika
helmet ['helmət]	Helm
racket ['rækɪt]	Schläger *(Tennis-)*
umpire ['ʌmpaɪə]	Schiedsrichter / -in
court [kɔ:t]	Spielfeld
ice hockey ['aɪs ˌhɒki]	Eishockey

race [reɪs]	Wettlauf, Rennen
brake [breɪk]	Bremse

Language 1: A new trick

event [ɪ'vent]	Ereignis, Veranstaltung
chance [tʃɑ:ns]	Chance; Gelegenheit, Möglichkeit
arrangement [ə'reɪndʒmənt]	Abmachung, Vereinbarung; Plan
feeling ['fi:lɪŋ]	Gefühl
not until [nɒt ʌn'tɪl]	erst (dann), wenn
to **offer** ['ɒfə]	(an)bieten
to **open** ['əʊpn]	eröffnen
situation [ˌsɪtju'eɪʃn]	Situation

Talkwise: Is it important to win?

talkwise ['tɔ:kwaɪz]	„redegewandt"
agreeing [ə'gri:ɪŋ]	Zustimmen
disagreeing [ˌdɪsə'gri:ɪŋ]	nicht zustimmen
wheelchair ['wi:ltʃeə]	Rollstuhl
once [wʌns]	einmal
to **agree** [ə'gri:]	zustimmen
exactly [ɪg'zæktli]	genau
rubbish ['rʌbɪʃ]	Unsinn, Quatsch; Müll; Gerümpel
luck [lʌk]	Glück

Language 2: Did you know?

relative clause [ˌrelətɪv 'klɔ:z]	Relativsatz
which [wɪtʃ]	der, dem, den, die, das *(Relativpronomen)*
American football [əˌmerɪkən 'fʊtbɔ:l]	American Football
half pl. **halves** [hɑ:f; hɑ:vz]	(die) Hälfte; Halbzeit
channel ['tʃænl]	Kanal; Programm

that [ðæt; ðət]	der, dem, den, die, das *(Relativpronomen)*
commercial break [kəˌmɜːʃl ˈbreɪk]	Werbepause
commercial [kəˈmɜːʃl]	Werbespot
who [huː]	der, dem, den, die *(Relativpronomen)*
also [ˈɔːlsəʊ]	auch
unusual [ʌnˈjuːʒl]	ungewöhnlich
bobsleigh [ˈbɒbsleɪ]	Bob
snow [snəʊ]	Schnee
whose [huːz]	dessen, deren *(Relativpronomen)*
rowing [ˈrəʊɪŋ]	Rudern
the lungs *(pl.)* [lʌŋz]	die Lunge
swimming [ˈswɪmɪŋ]	Schwimmen
scientist [ˈsaɪəntɪst]	Wissenschaftler / -in
disabled [dɪˈseɪbld]	behindert
athlete [ˈæθliːt]	(Leicht)Athlet / -in
gold medal [gəʊld ˈmedl]	Goldmedaille
record [ˈrekɔːd]	Rekord
marathon [ˈmærəθn]	Marathon
love [lʌv]	null *(Tennis)*
relative pronoun [ˌrelətɪv ˈprəʊnaʊn]	Relativpronomen
sweat [swet]	Schweiß
oddity [ˈɒdɪti]	Eigenartigkeit, Kuriosität
definition [ˌdefɪˈnɪʃn]	Definition
contact clause [ˈkɒntækt ˌklɔːz]	*Relativsatz ohne Relativpronomen*
exact [ɪgˈzækt]	genau, exakt

Text: Eddie the Eagle

eagle [ˈiːgl]	Adler
glasses *(pl.)* [ˈglɑːsɪz]	Brille

ski jump ['ski: dʒʌmp]	Skispringen
ski [ski:]	Ski
jump [dʒʌmp]	Sprung
at last [ət 'lɑ:st]	endlich, zu guter Letzt
press conference ['pres ˌkɒnfrns]	Pressekonferenz
to **mist up** [mɪst‿'ʌp]	(sich) beschlagen
goggles *(pl.)* ['gɒglz]	Skibrille, Schwimmbrille
ski jumper ['ski: ˌdʒʌmpə]	Skispringer
van [væn]	Lieferwagen, Transporter
tradition [trə'dɪʃn]	Tradition
far [fɑ:]	weit
might [maɪt]	könnte(n)
to **slide, slid, slid** [slaɪd, slɪd, slɪd]	gleiten; rutschen
to **flap** [flæp]	flattern, *(mit den Flügeln)* schlagen
place [pleɪs]	Platz
to **wave** [weɪv]	winken

Skills: Vocabulary skills – Using a German-English dictionary

context ['kɒntekst]	Kontext, Zusammenhang

1 Sports

Which letters are missing? Write down the complete words.

1. r ___ g ___ y
2. c ___ ic ___ et
3. ___ e ___ e ___ ee
4. t ___ a ___ k
5. ___ our ___
6. a ___ hle ___ i ___ s
7. ___ mpi ___ e
8. ra ___ k ___ t

2 Nouns

Fill in the crossword.

Down: ↓
1. Zustimmen
3. Situation
4. Ereignis, Veranstaltung
6. Platz

Across: →
2. Unsinn, Quatsch; Müll
5. Definition
7. Wettlauf, Rennen
8. Gefühl

3 Odd one out

Which word doesn't fit with the others?

1. skateboarding	rowing	swimming
2. ice hockey	American football	ski jump
3. ice	snow	sweat
4. athlete	scientist	eagle
5. commercial	gold medal	channel
6. tradition	unusual	oddity
7. brake	stick	bat
8. to go on	to open	to stop

4 Baseball

Which baseball words do you know?

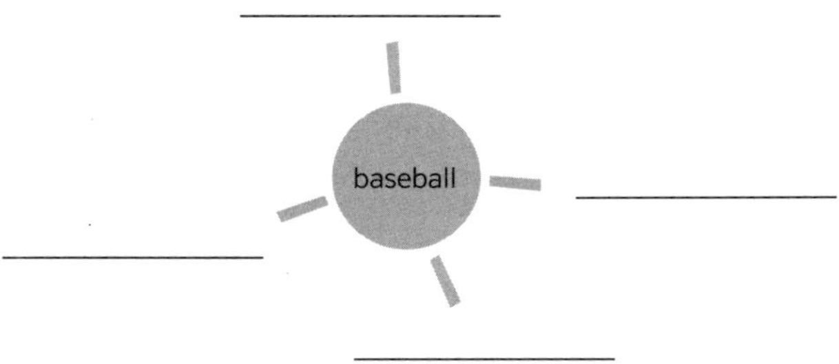

5 The letter 'o'

All of these words have the letter 'o' in them, but they aren't always pronounced in the same way. Sort the words.

bobsleigh · record · once · oval · oddity · snow · love · rowing · goggles · gold medal · skateboarding

[əʊ]	[ɒ]
____________	____________
____________	____________

[ɔː]	[ʌ]
____________	____________
____________	____________

6 Little words

Write down these words in English.

1. einmal ________________ 4. weit ________________

2. genau ________________ 5. könnte(n) ________________

3. auch ________________ 6. erst, wenn ________________

7 Plurals

What is the plural of these nouns?

1. glasses ________________ 4. pitch ________________

2. chance ________________ 5. event ________________

3. half ________________ 6. lungs ________________

8 Words for pictures

Find the right words for the pictures.

1. ________________________________

2. ________________________________

3. ________________________________

4. ________________________________

5. ________________________________

9 Verbs

Add an "-ing" to the words to make the progressive form.

1. to control ____________________
2. to slide ____________________
3. to flap ____________________
4. to wave ____________________
5. to go on ____________________
6. to open ____________________
7. to agree ____________________

10 Sports

In this unit you have read about many different sports. Can you remember all of them? Write them down.

____

____

____

____

____

11 Difficult words

Which words were you able to remember easily?

Which words do you still find difficult?
Write them down and repeat them.

LERNTIPP

Nicht die Dauer des Lernens ist wichtig, sondern die Regelmäßigkeit: Nimm Dir täglich 15 Minuten zum Vokabellernen. So kannst du die Wörter ohne Stress besser im Gedächtnis behalten.

Unit 2 Once upon a time …

Check-in

Once upon a time … ['wʌns‿ə,pɒn‿ə 'taɪm]	Es war einmal …
elephant ['elɪfənt]	Elefant
steel [sti:l]	Stahl
AD (= Anno Domini) [eɪ'di:]	nach Christus
Salve! *(lat. Begrüßung)* ['sælveɪ]	Sei gegrüßt!
to **keep out** [ki:p‿'aʊt]	draußen halten; draußen bleiben
century ['sentʃri]	Jahrhundert
invention [ɪn'venʃn]	Erfindung
wood [wʊd]	Holz
Valete! *(lat. Gruß zum Abschied)* [vəl'eɪti]	Es soll Euch gut gehen!
heir [eə]	Erbe, Erbin
to **attack** [ə'tæk]	angreifen
Bonjour! *(frz. Begrüßung)* [bɒŋ'ʒʊə]	Guten Tag!
Norman ['nɔ:mən]	Normanne, Normannin; normannisch
knight [naɪt]	Ritter
Saxon ['sæksn]	Sachse, Sächsin; sächsisch
to **hate** [heɪt]	hassen, nicht mögen
Bonjour, mes petits. [bɒŋ'ʒʊə meɪ pə,ti:]	Guten Tag, meine Kleinen.

Catholic ['kæθlɪk]	Katholik / -in; katholisch
Protestant ['prɒtɪstnt]	Protestant / -in; protestantisch
gold [gəʊld]	Gold
fave *(= favourite)* [feɪv]	Lieblings-
Hasta luego! *(Sp.)* [ˌʌstə lʊ'eɪgəʊ]	Bis später! *(Spanisch)*
to **defeat** [dɪ'fi:t]	besiegen
Elizabethan [ɪˌlɪzə'bi:θn]	elisabethanisch
age [eɪdʒ]	Zeitalter; Alter
poet ['pəʊɪt]	Dichter / -in
Romeo, wherefore art thou Romeo? ['rəʊmiəʊ ˌweəfɔ: 'ɑ:t ðaʊ]	Romeo, warum musst du nur Romeo sein?
Industrial Revolution [ɪnˌdʌstriəl rev'lu:ʃn]	Industrielle Revolution
factory ['fæktri]	Fabrik; Werk
steam engine ['sti:m ˌendʒɪn]	Dampfmaschine
power ['paʊə]	Strom, Elektrizität, Energie
workshop ['wɜ:kʃɒp]	Werkstatt; Workshop
empire ['empaɪə]	Reich; Kaiserreich
colony ['kɒləni]	Kolonie
World War II [ˌwɜ:ld ˌwɔ: 'tu:]	der Zweite Weltkrieg
independent [ˌɪndɪ'pendənt]	unabhängig
European Union [ˌjʊərəˌpi:ən 'ju:njən]	Europäische Union

Language 1: Visit the World Stage

Briton ['brɪtn]	Brite, Britin
stage [steɪdʒ]	Bühne
wax [wæks]	Wachs
dress [dres]	Kleid
to **be able to (do sth)** [bi‿'eɪbl tə]	können, fähig sein (zu)
No way! [ˌnəʊ 'weɪ]	Was?! / Echt?! / Nie im Leben!
to **be allowed to (do sth)** [bi‿ə'laʊd tə]	dürfen
modern ['mɒdn]	modern

action ['ækʃn]	Handlung; Action
to **have to** ['hæv tə]	müssen
negative ['negətɪv]	Verneinungsform
the following [ðə 'fɒləʊɪŋ]	folgende / -r / -s

Talkwise: Planning a special event

making suggestions [ˌmeɪkɪŋ sə'dʒestʃnz]	Vorschläge machen
suggestion [sə'dʒestʃn]	Vorschlag
to **suggest** [sə'dʒest]	vorschlagen
ought to ['ɔ:t‿tə]	sollte(n)
open day [ˌəʊpn 'deɪ]	Tag der offenen Tür
to **prepare** [prɪ'peə]	vorbereiten; zubereiten

Language 2: Get the facts: Victorian Britain

Victorian [vɪk'tɔ:riən]	viktorianisch; Viktorianer / -in
hot [hɒt]	heiß; gefragt
reign [reɪn]	Herrschaft
throne [θrəʊn]	Thron
raw material [ˌrɔ: mə'tɪəriəl]	Rohstoff
empress ['emprəs]	Kaiserin
farmer ['fɑ:mə]	Farmer / -in, Landwirt / -in
slum [slʌm]	Slum, Elendsviertel
clean [kli:n]	sauber
floor [flɔ:]	Fußboden
government ['gʌvnmənt]	Regierung
free [fri:]	kostenlos
past perfect [ˌpɑ:st 'pɜ:fɪkt]	Plusquamperfekt
fortress ['fɔ:trəs]	Festung
prison ['prɪzn]	Gefängnis
tower ['taʊə]	Turm

Skills: Reading skills – A historical story

to **get ready** [get 'redi]	sich vorbereiten; sich fertig machen
gist [dʒɪst]	das Wesentliche
detail ['di:teɪl]	Detail, Einzelheit
pre-reading [pri:'ri:dɪŋ]	vor dem Lesen
to **be about** [bi ə'baʊt]	gehen um, handeln von
to **be connected** [bi kə'nektɪd]	zusammenhängen, in Zusammenhang stehen
connecting line [kə'nektɪŋ ˌlaɪn]	Verbindungslinie
close [kləʊs]	genau; nahe

Text: The diary

girlfriend ['gɜ:lfrend]	Freundin *(in einer Paarbeziehung)*
jewellery ['dʒu:əlri]	Schmuck
old-fashioned [əʊld'fæʃnd]	altmodisch
lord [lɔ:d]	Lord, Herr
lady ['leɪdi]	Dame; Frau
middle name ['mɪdl ˌneɪm]	zweiter Vorname
to **joke** [dʒəʊk]	scherzen
servant ['sɜ:vnt]	Bedienstete / -r; Diener / -in
to **feed** [fi:d]	ernähren
lonely ['ləʊnli]	einsam
to **reply** [rɪ'plaɪ]	antworten, erwidern, entgegnen
to **shine, shone, shone** [ʃaɪn, ʃɒn, ʃɒn]	scheinen; glänzen
curious ['kjʊəriəs]	neugierig
to **clean** [kli:n]	säubern, reinigen
fountain ['faʊntɪn]	Springbrunnen
strange [streɪndʒ]	merkwürdig, seltsam; fremd
odd [ɒd]	seltsam, komisch
vision ['vɪʒn]	Vision
telegram ['telɪgræm]	Telegramm

to **drown** [draʊn]	ertrinken; ertränken
to **gasp** [gɑːsp]	tief einatmen, tief Luft holen; keuchen
such [sʌtʃ]	solche / -r / -s
sixth sense [ˌsɪksθ 'sens]	sechster Sinn
to **continue** [kən'tɪnjuː]	weiterreden; weitermachen
to **nod** [nɒd]	nicken
to **wonder** ['wʌndə]	sich fragen
ghost [gəʊst]	Geist
great-great-grandmother [ˌgreɪtgreɪt'grænmʌðə]	Urgroßmutter
whoever [huː'evə]	wer auch immer
wherever [weə'revə]	wo(hin) auch immer, egal wo(hin)
metal ['metl]	Metall
flying ['flaɪɪŋ]	fliegend, Flug-
actually ['æktʃuəli]	tatsächlich, wirklich; eigentlich
click [klɪk]	Klicken; Klick
line [laɪn]	(Telefon)leitung
to **have no idea** [hæv ˌnəʊ‿aɪ'dɪə]	keine Ahnung haben
paragraph ['pærəgrɑːf]	Paragraph, Absatz

Wordwise

stress [stres]	Betonung
to **stress** [stres]	betonen, hervorheben

1 Who am I?

What are the words? When you find the correct words and pick the right letters, you get a person.

bhaneeatzli ______________________ (6th letter: ___)

tttpesnaro ______________________ (2nd letter: ___)

ilahtocc ______________________ (7th letter: ___)

rtovcinai ______________________ (4th letter: ___)

oansx ______________________ (4th letter: ___)

noranm ______________________ (last letter: ___)

"I am a ______________________."

2 Languages

How could you say these things in English? Cross out the wrong sentences.

1. Salve! :	Hi!	No way!
2. Valete! :	Get lost!	Bye!
3. Hasta Luego! :	Nice to meet you!	See you later!
4. Bonjour! :	Hello!	Goodbye!

3 Compounds

Which words go together? Draw lines.

steam	line
raw	Revolution
Industrial	name
middle	day
European	material
connecting	engine
open	Union

4 Word rhymes

Which words from the unit rhyme with these words?

feel	____________	knee	____________
could	____________	mist	____________
hour	____________	need	____________
page	____________	fine	____________
door	____________	battle	____________

5 Opposites

Write down the opposites of these words.

to love ↔ ______________________

to be separate ↔ ______________________

to be serious ↔ ______________________

to ask ↔ ______________________

to mess up ↔ ______________________

to swim ↔ ______________________

to stop ↔ ______________________

to shake one's head ↔ ______________________

to stay in ↔ ______________________

to know ↔ ______________________

6 Adjectives

Put in the correct adjectives.

old-fashioned | odd | fave | lonely | close | negative | curious | modern | independent

1. That's my ________________ movie. I love it!
2. India didn't become ________________ until 1947.
3. This is a ________________ version of 'Romeo and Juliet'.
4. Don't be so ________________. Look on the bright side!
5. These old clothes would look ________________ on modern people.
6. After his wife had died he was very ________________.
7. I'm really ________________ about that new TV show.
8. We can walk to the castle. It's really ________________.
9. The clothes my mother wears are so ________________. She should buy some new ones.

7 Word groups

Sort the words into the right groups.

to attack | century | poet | prison | empress
to defeat | AD | tower | heir | age
knight | fortress | farmer

buildings	war	time	people

8 Modals

Which sentence is true?

1. I ought to go home.
   a) I'm still at the party.
   b) I'm already at home.

2. I'm allowed to cook dinner.
   a) My mother wants to cook.
   b) She lets me cook.

3. I had to listen to Dave's music.
   a) I could choose to listen.
   b) I couldn't choose.

4. I was able to find Lucy.
   a) I wanted to find her.
   b) I could find her.

9 Word puzzle

Find 15 words in the puzzle. ↓↑←→↘↙

gold, action, suggestion, slum, detail, jewellery, fountain, strange, such, actually, line, click, invention, clean, hot

T	A	C	T	U	A	L	L	Y	V
H	C	U	S	L	G	I	W	S	G
Y	T	E	S	X	F	N	Q	U	O
R	I	P	T	L	O	E	B	G	L
E	O	L	R	A	U	F	H	G	D
L	N	U	A	I	N	M	O	E	P
L	R	K	N	V	T	W	T	S	C
E	Z	C	G	H	A	A	R	T	V
W	E	I	E	Q	I	U	M	I	N
E	G	L	R	L	N	D	A	O	Y
J	D	C	F	C	L	E	A	N	O
P	I	N	V	E	N	T	I	O	N

10 Odd one out

Which word doesn't fit? Underline it.

1. stress	wax	dress
2. to prepare	to get ready	to gasp
3. servant	lord	lady
4. ghost	workshop	vision
5. factory	throne	reign
6. colony	empire	telegram

11 Hard or easy?

I thought these words in Unit 2 were …

easy	difficult

12 Words for tomorrow

I want to repeat these words tomorrow.

LERNTIPP

Versuche, bis zum nächsten Test einen typischen Fehler zu „verlernen“, der dir immer wieder passiert.

Unit 3 Living together

Check-in

to **meet** [mi:t]	kennenlernen
wise [waɪz]	weise
to **brush one's teeth** [brʌʃ wʌnz ˈti:θ]	(seine) Zähne putzen
or [ɔ:]	sonst
pip [pɪp]	Kern
to **grow, grew, grown** [grəʊ, gru:, grəʊn]	wachsen
to **eat up** [i:t ˈʌp]	aufessen
crust [krʌst]	Kruste, Rinde
to **go curly** [gəʊ ˈkɜ:li]	sich kräuseln
to **marry** [ˈmæri]	heiraten
bad luck [bæd ˈlʌk]	Pech, Unglück
hat [hæt]	Hut
to **tell a lie** [ˌtel‿ə ˈlaɪ]	lügen
lie [laɪ]	Lüge
(not) any more [nɒt ˌeni ˈmɔ:]	(nicht) mehr
vegetarian [ˌvedʒɪˈteəriən]	Vegetarier / -in
to **split up, split, split** [splɪt‿ˈʌp, splɪt, splɪt]	sich trennen
to **get on** [get‿ˈɒn]	auskommen
to **behave** [bɪˈheɪv]	sich benehmen, sich verhalten
twin [twɪn]	Zwilling, Zwillings-
to **drive someone crazy** [draɪv ˌsʌmwʌn ˈkreɪzi]	jmdn. verrückt machen
selfish [ˈselfɪʃ]	selbstsüchtig
to **tidy (up)** [taɪdi ˈʌp]	aufräumen, in Ordnung bringen

2L8 (= too late) [tuː ˈleɪt]	zu spät *(Abkürzung in SMS oder E-Mail)*
UR (= you are) [juː ˈɑː]	du bist *(Abkürzung in SMS oder E-Mail)*
I don't care! [aɪ ˌdəʊnt ˈkeə]	Das ist mir egal!
microwave [ˈmaɪkrəʊweɪv]	Mikrowelle
frozen [ˈfrəʊzn]	(tief)gefroren
Brussels sprout [ˌbrʌslz ˈspraʊt]	Rosenkohl
DIY (= Do-it-yourself) [ˌdiːaɪˈwaɪ]	Heimwerken
scene [siːn]	Szene
in [ɪn]	aus, von, jede / -r / -s (zweite / dritte …)
each other [iːtʃ‿ˈʌðə]	einander, sich (gegenseitig)
telephone [ˈtelɪfəʊn]	Telefon
cleaning lady [ˈkliːnɪŋ ˌleɪdi]	Putzfrau
answerphone [ˈɑːnsəfəʊn]	Anrufbeantworter

Language 1: Sunday lunch

to **enjoy oneself** [ɪnˈdʒɔɪ]	Spaß haben; sich amüsieren
himself [hɪmˈself]	selber
to **help oneself (to)** [help wʌnˈself tə]	sich bedienen
themselves [ðəmˈselvz]	selber
to **decide** [dɪˈsaɪd]	(sich) entscheiden
yourself [jɔːˈself]	selber
extra [ˈekstrə]	mehr
to **stand** [stænd]	ertragen, ausstehen
myself [maɪˈself]	selbst
yourselves [jɔːˈselvz]	selber
to **get dressed** [get ˈdrest]	sich anziehen
old people's home [əʊld ˈpiːplz həʊm]	Altersheim
to **relax** [rɪˈlæks]	(sich) entspannen, (sich) ausruhen; sich beruhigen
ourselves [aʊəˈselvz]	selber
reflexive [rɪˈfleksɪv]	reflexiv

herself [hɜːˈself]	selber
to **turn off** [tɜːn‿ˈɒf]	abschalten, ausschalten
itself [ɪtˈself]	selbst
to **call** [kɔːl]	anrufen

Watch out!
Many words are used with a reflexive pronoun in German, but not in English.

sich anstrengen	to **try hard**
sich anstellen	to **queue**
sich anziehen	to **get dressed**
sich etw. ausdenken	to **think of** sth
sich etw. ausleihen	to **borrow** sth
sich beeilen	to **hurry**
sich benehmen	to **behave**
sich bewegen	to **move**
sich entscheiden	to **decide**
sich entspannen	to **relax**
sich an etw. erinnern	to **remember** sth
sich fragen	to **wonder**
sich fühlen	to **feel**
sich an etw. gewöhnen	to **get used to** sth
sich Notizen machen	to **take notes**
sich (hin)setzen	to **sit down**
sich um etw. Sorgen machen	to **worry about** sth
sich treffen	to **meet**
sich trennen	to **split up**
sich verbessern	to **improve**
sich verirren	to **get lost**
sich verlieben	to **fall in love**
sich verstecken	to **hide**
sich vorstellen	to **imagine**

Talkwise: Meet halfway

to **meet halfway** [mi:t hɑ:f'weɪ]	(sich auf halbem Weg) entgegenkommen
to **feel sorry for** [fi:l 'sɒri]	Mitleid haben mit; bedauern
difference ['dɪfrns]	Unterschied
to **earn** [ɜ:n]	verdienen
I see. [aɪ 'si:]	Ich verstehe. / Aha!
to **mind** [maɪnd]	etwas dagegen haben; einem etwas ausmachen
You've got a point. [ju:v gɒt‿ə 'pɔɪnt]	Da ist was dran.

Language 2: Chatroom messages

type [taɪp]	Typ, Art, Sorte
to **chat** [tʃæt]	chatten; plaudern
to **turn into** [tɜ:n‿'ɪntə]	(sich) verwandeln in; werden
to **get rid of** [get 'rɪd‿əv]	loswerden
junk [dʒʌŋk]	Gerümpel; Ramsch
to **wish** [wɪʃ]	(sich) wünschen
jealous (of) ['dʒeləs‿əv]	neidisch; eifersüchtig
especially [ɪ'speʃli]	besonders, vor allem
probably ['prɒbəbli]	möglicherweise, wahrscheinlich
to **translate** [trænz'leɪt]	übersetzen
on chat [ɒn 'tʃæt]	im Chat, beim Chatten
purse [pɜ:s]	Geldbeutel
comma ['kɒmə]	Komma
advice [əd'vaɪs]	Rat, Ratschlag
difficult ['dɪfɪklt]	schwierig
wish [wɪʃ]	Wunsch

Language 3: A letter to an agony aunt

agony aunt ['ægəni ˌɑ:nt]	Kummerkastentante
boyfriend ['bɔɪfrend]	Freund *(in einer Paarbeziehung)*

to **go out with** [gəʊ‿'aʊt wɪð]	(aus)gehen mit
to **go crazy** [gəʊ 'kreɪzi]	ausflippen, durchdrehen
secret ['si:krət]	geheim
to **listen to** ['lɪsn tə]	hören auf

Skills: Listening Skills – Telephone messages

difficult ['dɪfɪklt]	schwierig
voice mail ['vɔɪs meɪl]	Voicemail; Mailbox
caller ['kɔ:lə]	Anrufer / -in
to **contact** ['kɒntækt]	(telefonisch) erreichen, sich in Verbindung setzen
to **leave** [li:v]	hinterlassen
to **take a call** [ˌteɪk‿ə 'kɔ:l]	(Telefon) abheben, einen Anruf entgegennehmen
tone [təʊn]	(Signal)ton
I'm afraid [aɪm ə'freɪd]	leider
to **be in** [bi‿'ɪn]	da sein

Text: Home alone

Home alone. [həʊm ə'ləʊn]	Allein zu Hause.
cast [kɑ:st]	Besetzung, Ensemble
Shut up! [ʃʌt‿'ʌp]	Halt die Klappe!
witch [wɪtʃ]	Hexe
costume ['kɒstju:m]	Kostüm
grumpy ['grʌmpi]	mürrisch, schlecht gelaunt
to **manage (to do sth)** ['mænɪdʒ]	(es) schaffen (etw. zu tun)
talk [tɔ:k]	Gespräch, Unterhaltung; Unterredung
to **make a decision** [ˌmeɪk‿ə dɪ'sɪʒn]	eine Entscheidung treffen
decision [dɪ'sɪʒn]	Entscheidung
to **get in the way** [ˌget‿ɪn ðə 'weɪ]	stören, im Weg stehen
to **make sure** [meɪk 'ʃɔ:]	sich versichern
mask [mɑ:sk]	Maske

First things first. [ˌfɜ:st θɪŋz ˈfɜ:st]	Das Wichtigste zuerst.
doorbell [ˈdɔ:bel]	Türklingel
What's going on? [wɒts ˌɡəʊɪŋ‿ˈɒn]	Was ist denn hier los?
guy [ɡaɪ]	Typ, Kerl; *pl.* Leute
one by one [ˌwʌn baɪ ˈwʌn]	eine / -r / -s nach dem / der anderen
to **react** [riˈækt]	reagieren
to **put on (a play)** [ˌpʊt‿ɒn‿ə ˈpleɪ]	(ein Theaterstück) aufführen
director [dɪˈrektə]	Regisseur / -in
props *(pl.)* [prɒps]	Requisiten
lights *(pl.)* [laɪts]	Beleuchtung
programme [ˈprəʊɡræm]	Programmheft
actress [ˈæktrəs]	Schauspielerin
rehearsal [rɪˈhɜ:sl]	Probe
to **rehearse** [rɪˈhɜ:s]	proben
curtain [ˈkɜ:tn]	Vorhang
audience [ˈɔ:diəns]	Publikum
to **applaud** [əˈplɔ:d]	applaudieren
author [ˈɔ:θə]	Autor / -in

Wordwise

official [əˈfɪʃl]	offiziell

1 Verbs

Which words go together? Draw lines. Then make a sentence with each verb.

to eat	on	______________________
to get	with	______________________
to tidy	into	______________________
to turn	of	______________________
to get rid	to	______________________
to go out	up	______________________
to listen	on	______________________
to put	up	______________________

2 Irregular Verbs

Complete the grid.

to meet		
	split up	
		stood
	felt	
to leave		
		grown
	ate up	
to get on		

3 Wordsnake

How many hidden words are there in the wordsnake?

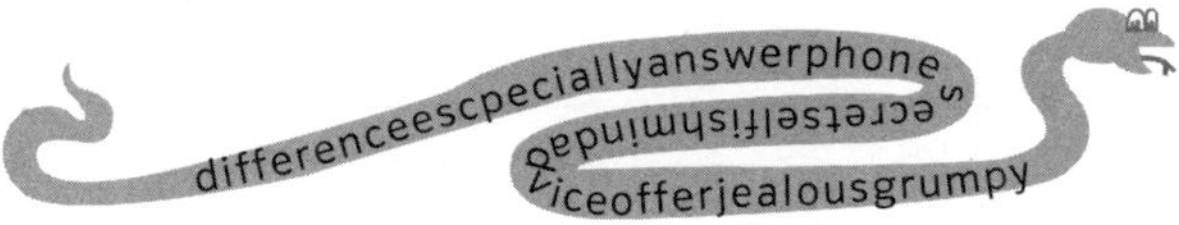

____

____

____

____

4 Theatre

Fill in the crossword with these theatre words.

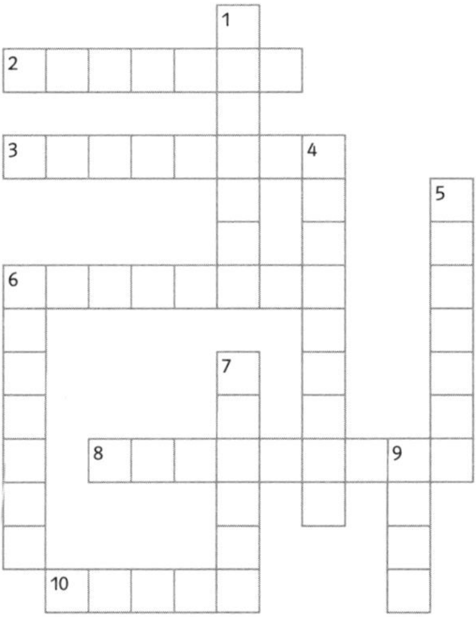

Down: ↓

1. Vorhang
4. Probe
5. Kostüm
6. Schauspielerin
7. Beleuchtung
9. Maske

Across: →

2. applaudieren
3. Regisseur
6. Publikum
8. Programmheft
10. Requisiten

5 Reflexive pronouns

Put in the correct reflexive pronoun.

1. I wash ______________________________.
2. You dress ______________________________.
3. He feeds ______________________________.
4. She scares ______________________________.
5. It explains ______________________________.
6. We help ______________________________.
7. You all love ______________________________.
8. They hurt ______________________________.

6 Opposites

Write down the opposites of these words.

1. to divorce ↔ ______________________
2. foolish ↔ ______________________
3. good luck ↔ ______________________
4. to tell the truth ↔ ______________________
5. still ↔ ______________________
6. fried ↔ ______________________
7. easy ↔ ______________________

7 Words for pictures

Find the right words for the pictures.

1. ____________________________________

2. ____________________________________

3. ____________________________________

4. ____________________________________

5. ____________________________________

8 Which word?

1. [wɪʃ]	a) wish	b) which
2. [təʊn]	a) town	b) tone
3. [grəʊ]	a) grey	b) grow
4. [hæt]	a) hat	b) head
5. [laɪ]	a) lay	b) lie
6. [tʃæt]	a) chat	b) shed
7. [pɜːs]	a) purse	b) pause
8. [ˈkɔːlə]	a) colour	b) caller

9 Expressions

How do you say these sentences in English?

1. Halt die Klappe! ______________________________
2. Du machst mich verrückt! ______________________________

   ____
3. Bedien dich. ______________________________
4. Ich verstehe. ______________________________
5. Da ist was dran. ______________________________
6. Amüsiert euch! ______________________________
7. Ich kann leider nicht kommen. ______________________________

   ____
8. Was ist denn hier los? ______________________________
9. Das Wichtigste zuerst. ______________________________
10. Das ist mir egal! ______________________________

10 Choose the right word

Which of the words on the right goes with those on the left?

1. to comb one's hair	a) to go curly
to wash	b) to brush one's teeth
2. egg	a) Brussels sprout
apple	b) mobile
3. to want	a) to wish
to dream	b) mobile
4. kind	a) scene
sort	b) type
5. to contact	a) to turn off
to meet halfway	b) to call
6. agony aunt	a) cleaning lady
boyfriend	b) doorbell
7. to manage	a) to get in the way
to make a decision	b) to make sure

11 New words

I thought these words in Unit 4 were …

difficult to remember	easy to remember	useful

LERNTIPP

Schaffe dir zum Lernen ein positives Umfeld. An einem aufgeräumten Schreibtisch lässt es sich besser lernen und auch eine angenehme Beleuchtung kann helfen. Versuche auch, störende Einflüsse wie einen lauten Fernseher zu vermeiden.

Unit 4 The UK on the move

Check-in

to **be on the move** [bi ɒn‿ðə 'mu:v]	unterwegs sein
on average [ɒn‿'ævrɪdʒ]	durchschnittlich, im Durchschnitt
to **move (house)** [mu:v 'haʊs]	umziehen
perhaps [pə'hæps]	vielleicht
exchange [ɪks'tʃeɪndʒ]	Austausch
region ['ri:dʒn]	Region; Gegend
industry ['ɪndəstri]	Industrie, Industrieanlage
cult [kʌlt]	Kult
birthplace ['bɜ:θpleɪs]	Geburtsort
recently ['ri:sntli]	kürzlich, vor kurzem, neulich; in letzter Zeit
facelift ['feɪslɪft]	Lifting; *hier:* Renovierung, Verschönerung
landscape ['lændskeɪp]	Landschaft
Welsh [welʃ]	walisisch; Walisisch
to **be proud (of)** [bi 'praʊd‿əv]	stolz sein (auf)
regional ['ri:dʒnl]	regional
culture ['kʌltʃə]	Kultur
wing [wɪŋ]	Flügel
coal mine ['kəʊl maɪn]	Kohlenbergwerk, Kohlengrube
heavy industry [ˌhevi 'ɪndəstri]	Schwerindustrie

male voice choir [ˌmeɪl vɔɪs 'kwaɪə]	Männerchor
to **exist** [ɪg'zɪst]	bestehen
contrast ['kɒntrɑːst]	Kontrast, Unterschied
less [les]	weniger

Language 1: Welsh relatives

abstract ['æbstrækt]	abstrakt
article ['ɑːtɪkl]	Artikel *(gramm.)*
relative ['relətɪv]	Verwandte / -r
engineer [ˌendʒɪ'nɪə]	Ingenieur / -in
firm [fɜːm]	Firma
the poor [ðə 'pɔː]	die Armen
tea [tiː]	(frühes) Abendessen
friendship ['frendʃɪp]	Freundschaft
I'd rather [aɪd 'rɑːðə]	ich würde lieber
bilingual [baɪ'lɪŋgwl]	zweisprachig
love [lʌv]	Liebe
a pair of [ə 'peər‿əv]	ein Paar
taste [teɪst]	Geschmack
to **be into sth** [bi‿'ɪntə]	sich für etw. interessieren; etw. mögen
awful ['ɔːfl]	schrecklich, furchtbar
definite ['defɪnət]	bestimmt
indefinite [ɪn'defɪnət]	unbestimmt

Talkwise: Dealing with problems

helping ['helpɪŋ]	Helfen
apologizing [ə'pɒlədʒaɪzɪŋ]	Entschuldigen
dealing with problems [ˌdiːlɪŋ wɪð 'prɒbləmz]	Schwierigkeiten bewältigen
to **deal with, dealt, dealt** ['diːl wɪð, delt, delt]	sich befassen mit, umgehen mit
Take your time. [ˌteɪk jɔː 'taɪm]	Lass dir Zeit.
to **apologize** [ə'pɒlədʒaɪz]	sich entschuldigen

I didn't mean to … [aɪ ˌdɪdnt ˈmiːn tə]	Ich wollte nicht …
rude [ruːd]	unhöflich; unverschämt
Never mind! [ˌnevə ˈmaɪnd]	Schon gut.

Language 2: Up North

up North [ʌp ˈnɔːθ]	im Norden
Asian [ˈeɪʃn]	asiatisch; Asiate, Asiatin
curry [ˈkʌri]	Curry *(Gewürz oder Gericht)*
to **smell, smelt, smelt** [smel, smelt, smelt]	riechen; duften
to **taste** [teɪst]	schmecken
Punjabi [pʌnˈdʒɑːbiː]	Pandschabi; pandschabisch
to **sound** [saʊnd]	klingen
to **seem** [siːm]	scheinen
exhibition [ˌeksɪˈbɪʃn]	Ausstellung
by [baɪ]	*(spätestens)* bis
Bhangra [ˈbæŋɡrə]	Bhangra *(Musikstil, der Bestandteile der indischen und westlichen Musik in sich vereint)*
reply [rɪˈplaɪ]	Antwort
audio [ˈɔːdiəʊ]	Audio-, Hör-

Skills: Reading Skills – Factual texts

factual text [ˌfæktʃʊəl ˈtekst]	Sachtext
research [riːˈsɜːtʃ]	Recherche; Forschung; Untersuchung
skimming [ˈskɪmɪŋ]	Überfliegen
to **skim** [skɪm]	überfliegen
to **concentrate** [ˈkɒnsntreɪt]	(sich) konzentrieren
keyword [ˈkiːwɜːd]	Stichwort; Schlüsselbegriff
scanning [ˈskænɪŋ]	Durchsuchen nach Details; Abtasten

to **scan** [skæn]	durchsuchen, abtasten
topic ['tɒpɪk]	Thema
a must-see [ə ˌmʌst 'si:]	… muss man gesehen haben
conference ['kɒnfrns]	Konferenz, Tagung
dinner ['dɪnə]	Abendessen
leisure ['leʒə]	Freizeit, Freizeit-
on land [ɒn 'lænd]	an Land
during *(+ noun)* ['djʊərɪŋ]	während *(+ Substantiv)*
motorway ['məʊtəweɪ]	Autobahn

Text: Changing places

changing places [ˌtʃeɪndʒɪŋ 'pleɪsɪz]	Ortswechsel
It's a pity. [ˌɪts‿ə 'pɪti]	Das ist schade. / Es ist schade …
accent ['æksnt]	Akzent
to **get tired of** [get 'taɪəd‿əv]	etwas satt bekommen
interactive [ˌɪntər'æktɪv]	interaktiv
across [ə'krɒs]	herüber
for laughs [fə 'lɑ:fs]	zum Spaß
waterfront ['wɔ:təfrʌnt]	Hafenviertel; Ufer
weird [wɪəd]	merkwürdig, seltsam
crowd [kraʊd]	Menschenmenge
to **cheer** [tʃɪə]	(zu)jubeln, anfeuern
to **try out** [traɪ‿'aʊt]	ausprobieren
to **make fun of** [ˌmeɪk 'fʌn‿əv]	sich lustig machen über
quite [kwaɪt]	ziemlich; ganz, völlig
to **hang out (with), hung, hung** [ˌhæŋ 'aʊt wɪð, hʌŋ, hʌŋ]	sich treffen (mit); rumhängen (mit)
search engine ['sɜ:tʃ ˌendʒɪn]	Suchmaschine
at least [ət 'li:st]	mindestens, wenigstens

1 Missing words

Look at the words on the left to find the missing words.

1. much → more   little → ______
2. England → country   North West → ______
3. tree → nature   factory → ______
4. Scotland → Scottish   Wales → ______
5. horse → leg   bird → ______
6. perfume → smell   food → ______
7. France → European   China → ______
8. music → concert   art → ______
9. morning → breakfast   evening → ______
10. to watch → video   to listen → ______

2 Being polite

How can you reply to these sentences?

1. Hey, you pushed me! - Sorry, I ______.
2. I have to think about it. - That's OK. ______.
3. I'm sorry. Is that your chair? - Oh, no. ______.
4. I can't have dinner with you tonight. - ______.
5. Can you stay a bit longer? No, ______ go home now.

3 Phrasal verbs

Which verbs do you know from this Unit? Draw lines.

to be	of
to deal	out
to get tired	with
to make fun	into
to try	with
to hang out	of

4 Verbs

Put in the right verb.

1. We ________________ house last year.
2. You have to ________________ that problem by yourself.
3. Ghosts and monsters don't ________________.
4. I want to ________________ for being rude.
5. These flowers ________________ wonderful.
6. He ________________ to be a really nice guy.
7. The cake you baked ________________ awful!
8. This river ________________ into the sea.
9. Everyone ________________ when he won the match.

5 Definitions

Complete the sentences with words from the unit.

1. When you are as smart or talented as most other people, you are ____________________.
2. When you are travelling from one place to another, you are ____________________.
3. Something that becomes very popular for many people is a ____________________.
4. Reporters write this for a newspaper: ____________________
5. Your aunt, uncle and grandma are your ____________________.
6. A company is also called a ____________________.
7. We call people who haven't got much money ____________________.
8. When you speak two languages perfectly you are ____________________.
9. William Shakespeare was born in Stratford-upon-Avon. The town is his ____________________.

6 Picture Puzzle

Which words do the pictures show?

1. ______________________________

2. ______________________________

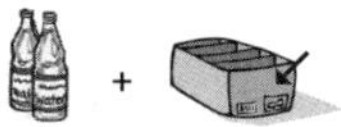

3. ______________________________

4. ______________________________

7 Little words

Put in the right words: quite, at least, recently, by, during

1. They ________________ opened a new café in town.
2. I will have done my homework ________________ tomorrow morning.
3. We listened to cool music ________________ the trip.
4. I can show you around the city. I know it ________________ well.
5. There were ________________ a hundred people on the square.

8 Two words in one

In these jumbled letters there are always two hidden words. Find them and write them down.

1. saatbrtteca ______________ ______________
2. pihecgllrnu ______________ ______________
3. peresleliryu ______________ ______________
4. ossrttmicnka ______________ ______________
5. uducwrrielet ______________ ______________
6. icetoccntpa ______________ ______________

9 Word friends

Make word pairs. Watch out! One word is written together, one word with a hyphen (-).

key, coal, must, factual, search, mine, see, engine, word, text

1. ______________________
2. ______________________
3. ______________________
4. ______________________
5. ______________________

10 Phonetics

Write down the words.

[ɪks'tʃeɪndʒ] ______________________________

['ri:dʒnl] ______________________________

[ˌendʒɪ'nɪə] ______________________________

['ɔ:fl] ______________________________

[ru:d] ______________________________

['kʌri] ______________________________

[ri:'sɜ:tʃ] ______________________________

[kraʊd] ______________________________

11 Just one minute

Look at the words from Unit 4 for one minute. Then write down all the words you can remember. After that check the spelling.

____

____

____

____

____

____

LERNTIPP

Lass dir für jede Vokabel genügend Zeit. Sprich die neue Vokabel mehrmals laut und deutlich vor dich hin. Präge dir jedes Wort gut ein.

Unit 5 Media messages

Check-in

medium pl. **media** ['mi:diəm, 'mi:diə]	Medium, Medien
celeb(rity) [sə'leb, sə'lebrɪti]	berühmte Persönlichkeit
to **copy** ['kɒpi]	nachmachen
to **change** [tʃeɪndʒ]	(sich) verändern
quality ['kwɒləti]	Qualität; Qualitäts-
popular newspaper [ˌpɒpjələ 'nju:sˌpeɪpə]	Boulevardzeitung
newspaper ['nju:sˌpeɪpə]	Zeitung
to **create** [kri'eɪt]	(er)schaffen
the public [ðə 'pʌblɪk]	die Öffentlichkeit
studio ['stju:diəʊ]	Studio
concert ['kɒnsət]	Konzert
awesome ['ɔ:səm]	super, spitze; beeindruckend
main [meɪn]	Haupt-
entertainment *(no pl.)* [ˌentə'teɪnmənt]	Unterhaltung
soap (opera) ['səʊp ˌɒprə]	Seifenoper, Soap
realistic [ˌrɪə'lɪstɪk]	realistisch
violence *(no pl.)* ['vaɪəlns]	Gewalt
housewife pl. **housewives** ['haʊswaɪf, 'haʊswaɪvz]	Hausfrau
to **advertise** ['ædvətaɪz]	Werbung machen (für), werben; anpreisen; inserieren

soap *(no pl.)* [səʊp]	Seife
cleaning product ['kli:nɪŋ ˌprɒdʌkt]	Reinigungsmittel, Putzmittel
nickname ['nɪkneɪm]	Spitzname
copy ['kɒpi]	Exemplar
programme ['prəʊgræm]	Programm; Sendung

Language 1: Casting for a daily soap

passive ['pæsɪv]	Passiv
to **discover** [dɪ'skʌvə]	entdecken
to **cast, cast, cast** [kɑ:st, kɑ:st, kɑ:st]	jmdm. eine Rolle (in einem Film) geben
agent ['eɪdʒnt]	Agent / -in
file [faɪl]	Akte
script [skrɪpt]	Drehbuch, Skript
sides [saɪdz]	Skript beim Casting
to **reread, reread, reread** [ri:'ri:d, ri:'red, ri:'red]	noch einmal lesen
Don't get your hopes up too high. [dəʊnt get jɔ: ˌhəʊps ʌp tu: 'haɪ]	Mach dir nicht zu viele Hoffnungen.
assistant [ə'sɪstnt]	Assistent / -in
to **sign** [saɪn]	unterschreiben
contract ['kɒntrækt]	Vertrag
super ['su:pə]	super
to **discuss** [dɪ'skʌs]	diskutieren
to **film** [fɪlm]	filmen, drehen
to **photograph** ['fəʊtəgrɑ:f]	fotografieren
active ['æktɪv]	Aktiv
by [baɪ]	von

False friends
Do you remember what false friends are? They are words which look or sound like German words, but have a different meaning in English. So watch out for these nouns and verbs!

action	Handlung	**note**	Notiz
art	Kunst	**personal**	persönlich
(to) **become**	werden	(to) **photograph**	fotografieren
city	Großstadt	**rock**	Fels, Stein
map	Stadtplan, Landkarte	**sea**	Meer, die See
meaning	Bedeutung	(to) **spend**	ausgeben
menu	Speisekarte	**trainers**	Turnschuhe

Talkwise: Talk about media in your life

discussing [dɪ'skʌsɪŋ]	Diskutieren
pros and cons *(pl.)* [ˌprəʊz‿n 'kɒnz]	Pro und Kontra
couch potato ['kaʊtʃ pəˌteɪtəʊ]	Fernsehglotzer / -in, Couchpotato
maniac ['meɪniæk]	Verrückte / -r, Wahnsinnige / -r
bookworm ['bʊkwɜ:m]	Bücherwurm

Language 2: Advertising

advertising *(no pl.)* ['ædvətaɪzɪŋ]	Werbung, Reklame
to **be worth (sth)** [bi 'wɜ:θ]	(etw.) wert sein
smooth [smu:θ]	glatt
look [lʊk]	Aussehen
tube [tju:b]	Tube
soccer ['sɒkə]	Fußball
product ['prɒdʌkt]	Produkt, Erzeugnis
ad(vertisement) [əd'vɜ:tɪsmənt]	Anzeige; Werbespot
headline ['hedlaɪn]	Schlagzeile

to **get sb's attention** [get ə'tenʃn]	jmdn. auf sich aufmerksam machen

Skills: Vocabulary Skills – Writing a newspaper report

LAN *(Local Area Network)* [læn; ˌləʊkl ˌeəriə 'netwɜ:k]	LAN
beginning [bɪ'gɪnɪŋ]	Anfang; Beginn
basic ['beɪsɪk]	grundlegend, Grund-; einfach
to **attend** [ə'tend]	teilnehmen, besuchen
to **organise** ['ɔ:gənaɪz]	organisieren
youth [ju:θ]	Jugend
to **raise money** [reɪz 'mʌni]	Geld sammeln, Geld aufbringen
argument ['ɑ:gjəmənt]	Auseinandersetzung, Streit
violent ['vaɪəlnt]	gewalttätig
noise [nɔɪz]	Lärm, Krach; Geräusch
background ['bækgraʊnd]	Hintergrund
police department [pə'li:s dɪˌpɑ:tmənt]	Polizeidienststelle
to **give one's opinion** [ˌgɪv wʌnz ə'pɪnjən]	seine Meinung äußern
opinion [ə'pɪnjən]	Meinung
to **allow** [ə'laʊ]	erlauben, gestatten
to **exchange** [ɪks'tʃeɪndʒ]	austauschen
to **rewrite** [ri:'raɪt]	umschreiben; neu schreiben

Text: No couch potatoes!

to convince [kən'vɪns]	überzeugen
cereal *(no pl.)* ['sɪəriəl]	Frühstückszerealie, Getreideprodukt *(z. B. Cornflakes oder Müsli)*
magic ['mædʒɪk]	Magie, Zauberei
to **get sb to do sth** ['get ˌsʌmbədi tə 'du: ˌsʌmθɪŋ]	jmdn. dazu bewegen, etwas zu tun
pile [paɪl]	Stapel, Haufen

to **fall off** [fɔ:l 'ɒf]	herunterfallen, (hinunter) fallen
ramp [ræmp]	Rampe
to **disappear** [ˌdɪsə'pɪə]	verschwinden
to **crack** [kræk]	(zer)brechen; (zer)springen
cold [kəʊld]	Erkältung
spinach *(no pl.)* ['spɪnɪtʃ]	Spinat
to **admit** [əd'mɪt]	zugeben
to **walk past** [wɔ:k 'pɑ:st]	vorbeigehen, vorbeilaufen
above [ə'bʌv]	oben, über, oberhalb
outline ['aʊtlaɪn]	Umriss, Silhouette
roof [ru:f]	Dach
to **cut, cut, cut** [kʌt, kʌt, kʌt]	(sich) schneiden
pipe [paɪp]	Rohr
gash [gæʃ]	tiefe Schnittwunde
blood [blʌd]	Blut
patient ['peɪʃnt]	Patient / -in
to **distract** [dɪ'strækt]	ablenken
bandage ['bændɪdʒ]	Verband
emergency [ɪ'mɜ:dʒnsi]	Notfall, Notlage
to **tie** [taɪ]	binden, zubinden
tight [taɪt]	fest, eng
ambulance ['æmbjələns]	Krankenwagen
to **rescue** ['reskju:]	retten
to **grow up** [grəʊ‿'ʌp]	erwachsen werden; aufwachsen

1 Words for pictures

Find the right words for the pictures.

1. ______________________________

2. ______________________________

3. ______________________________

4. ______________________________

5. ______________________________

2 Mixed words

Which verbs are hidden in these jumbled letters?

1. pyoc: to ____________________
2. acrkc: to ____________________
3. wlaol: to ____________________
4. ahgcne: to ____________________
5. reirtwe: to ____________________
6. orsaegni: to ____________________
7. neexcgha: to ____________________

3 Find the word

Write the words and find the thing that most people are looking for in the media.

1. The heading of an article:

   ______________________ (2nd + 7th letter:________)

2. The people films are made for:

   ______________________ (1st letter:________)

3. A famous person:

   ______________________ (4th + 6th letter:________)

4. Someone who watches TV all the time:

   ______________________ (8th + 9th letter:________)

5. The place where stars make films:

   ______________________ (5th letter:________)

6. A network which connects computers:

   ______________________ (3rd letter:________)

7. It's on TV or in a magazine and shows you a new product:

   ______________________ (10th + 11th letter:________)

8. An event where bands play their music for their fans:

   ______________________ (3rd + 7th letter:________)

The word is ______________________.

4 Verbs and nouns

Which nouns do the verbs go with? Draw lines.

to attend	a topic
to reread	a new star
to discuss	a horse
to create	a meeting
to cast	a script
to fall off	a new show

5 Word groups

Which topic do the words go with? Sort them.

to discover | ambulance | to tie | agent | sides
emergency | to sign | patient | blood | file
contract | bandage | script | to rescue

an accident	**a casting**
______________________	______________________
______________________	______________________
______________________	______________________
______________________	______________________
______________________	______________________

6 The same and different

Which word from Unit 5 means

a) *the same as …*

1. sound → ______________________
2. in a higher place → ______________________
3. great → ______________________
4. to take a picture → ______________________
5. to say what you think → ______________________

b) *the opposite of …*

1. active ↔ ______________________
2. ending ↔ ______________________
3. old age ↔ ______________________
4. to lose money ↔ ______________________
5. boss ↔ ______________________

7 Missing letters

Which letters are missing? Write down the complete words.

1. to f ___ l ___
2. to be w ___ rt ___
3. to ___ is ___ pp ___ ___ r
4. to ___ d ___ it
5. to ___ al ___ past
6. to ___ u ___
7. to d ___ st ___ a ___ t
8. to get ___ tt ___ nt ___ on

8 Word puzzle

Find the 12 nouns and 4 adjectives from the Unit in the word puzzle and write them down. ↑ ↓ ← → ↘ ↙

T	F	B	S	P	I	N	A	C	H	V	L
N	O	V	D	U	R	H	P	W	Q	I	S
R	O	R	I	Y	C	O	Z	D	L	O	C
E	R	M	S	O	T	U	D	K	F	L	E
A	B	O	C	G	L	S	E	U	X	E	R
L	M	U	U	L	B	E	O	R	C	N	E
I	V	T	S	A	T	W	N	E	N	T	A
S	F	L	S	P	I	I	R	C	W	B	L
T	V	I	I	R	G	F	Q	C	E	S	D
I	C	N	N	O	H	E	M	O	L	I	C
C	P	E	G	A	T	G	H	S	A	G	H
U	A	R	G	U	M	E	N	T	Y	T	F

9 Odd sound out

Which word is wrong in each line? Cross it out.

1.	[iː]	medium	nickname	cleaning product
2.	[ɒ]	programme	copy	quality
3.	[uː]	super	smooth	look
4.	[eɪ]	main	magic	maniac
5.	[æ]	ramp	above	background

10 Difficult words

Which words from this Unit did you find difficult?
Write them again.

____

____

____

LERNTIPP

Lass dich von der Anzahl neuer Vokabeln nicht abschrecken. Oft kannst du Wörter aus dem Deutschen herleiten, da sie ähnlich geschrieben oder ausgesprochen werden:

instrument – Instrument;
orchestra – Orchester

Unit 6 Time to travel

Check-in

traveller ['trævlə]	Reisende / -r
journey ['dʒɜ:ni]	Reise
noodle ['nu:dl]	Nudel
plant [plɑ:nt]	Pflanze
evolution [ˌi:və'lu:ʃn]	Evolution, Entwicklung
missionary ['mɪʃnri]	Missionar / -in
moon [mu:n]	Mond
step [step]	Schritt, Stufe
giant [dʒaɪənt]	Riesen-, riesig
leap [li:p]	Sprung, Satz
mankind [mæn'kaɪnd]	Menschheit
challenge ['tʃælɪndʒ]	Herausforderung
to **take** [teɪk]	dauern, (Zeit) brauchen
first language ['fɜ:st ˌlæŋgwɪdʒ]	Muttersprache
per cent [pə'sent]	Prozent

Language 1: To the ends of the earth

reporting what someone said [rɪˌpɔ:tɪŋ wɒt sʌmwʌn 'sed]	wiedergeben, was jemand gesagt hat
to **mention** ['menʃn]	erwähnen
disappointing [ˌdɪsə'pɔɪntɪŋ]	enttäuschend
to **get bored** [get 'bɔ:d]	sich langweilen
to **report** [rɪ'pɔ:t]	berichten, wiedergeben
to **introduce** [ˌɪntrə'dju:s]	einführen, einleiten

direct speech [ˌdɪrekt ˈspiːtʃ]	direkte Rede
indirect speech [ˌɪndɪrekt ˈspiːtʃ]	indirekte Rede
welcome [ˈwelkəm]	Empfang
two days earlier [ˌtuː deɪz ˈɜːliə]	vor zwei Tagen, zwei Tage zuvor
the day before [ðə ˌdeɪ bɪˈfɔː]	am Tag vorher, am Tag zuvor
to **ask about sb / sth** [ɑːsk əˈbaʊt]	sich nach jmdm. / etw. erkundigen

Talkwise: Read the book, watch the film, play the game

giving advice [ˌɡɪvɪŋ ədˈvaɪs]	einen Rat geben
biography [baɪˈɒɡrəfi]	Biografie
comedy [ˈkɒmədi]	Komödie
to **recommend** [ˌrekəˈmend]	empfehlen
Who's in it? [huːz ˈɪn‿ɪt]	Wer spielt mit?

Language 2: Emergency on the motorway

coach [kəʊtʃ]	Reisebus
police officer [pəˌliːs ˈɒfɪsə]	Polizeibeamte / -r
dangerous [ˈdeɪndʒrəs]	gefährlich
chemical [ˈkemɪkl]	Chemikalie
to **warn sb** [wɔːn]	jmdn. warnen; jmdn. ermahnen
service [ˈsɜːvɪs]	Service, Dienst; Verbindung *(Zug, Bus)*
paramedic [ˌpærəˈmedɪk]	Sanitäter / -in
whether [ˈweðə]	ob
firefighter [ˈfaɪəˌfaɪtə]	Feuerwehrmann, Feuerwehrfrau
area [ˈeəriə]	Areal; Fläche; Gebiet
to **advise (sb to do sth)** [ədˈvaɪz]	(jmdm.) raten (etw. zu tun)
command [kəˈmɑːnd]	Befehl
to **ask sb to do sth** [ˈɑːsk tə]	jmdn. bitten, etw. zu tun

burglar ['bɜːglə]	Einbrecher / -in
to **be trapped** [bi 'træpt]	eingeschlossen sein; in der Falle sitzen

Skills: Speaking Skills – Small talk

second language ['seknd ˌlæŋgwɪdʒ]	Zweitsprache
fantastic [fæn'tæstɪk]	fantastisch, großartig
Right? [raɪt]	Stimmt's? / Nicht wahr?
annoying [ə'nɔɪɪŋ]	ärgerlich; lästig
And you. [ənd 'juː]	Gleichfalls.
filler ['fɪlə]	Füllwort
extra ['ekstrə]	zusätzlich

Text: My big adventure

railway ['reɪlweɪ]	Eisenbahn
to **complete** [kəm'pliːt]	fertig stellen
seat [siːt]	Sitz, Sitzplatz
princess [prɪn'ses]	Prinzessin
to **save** [seɪv]	retten
track [træk]	Gleis; Spur
prairie ['preəri]	Prärie
to **slow down** [sləʊ 'daʊn]	langsamer werden
bellow ['beləʊ]	Gebrüll
to **jump out of one's skin** [ˌdʒʌmp‿aʊt‿əv wʌnz 'skɪn]	sich zu Tode erschrecken
skin [skɪn]	Haut; Fell
buffalo pl. buffalo ['bʌfləʊ]	Büffel
delay [dɪ'leɪ]	Verzögerung, Verspätung
bet [bet]	Wette
to **continue** [kən'tɪnjuː]	weitergehen, -fahren, -reisen
on foot [ɒn 'fʊt]	zu Fuß
to **take the chance** [ˌteɪk ðə 'tʃɑːns]	es darauf ankommen lassen, das Risiko eingehen
whistle ['wɪsl]	Pfiff, Pfeifen
to **make it** ['meɪk‿ɪt]	es schaffen

side [saɪd]	Seite
scream [skri:m]	Schrei
to **scream** [skri:m]	schreien, kreischen

Verbs and nouns with the same form

(to)	**drink**	trinken	(to)	**milk**	melken
	drink	Getränk		**milk**	Milch
(to)	**end**	enden	(to)	**paint**	(an)malen, streichen
	end	Ende		**paint**	Farbe
(to)	**fight**	kämpfen	(to)	**plan**	planen
	fight	Kampf		**plan**	Plan
(to)	**film**	filmen	(to)	**rain**	regnen
	film	Film		**rain**	Regen
(to)	**help**	helfen	(to)	**scream**	schreien, kreischen
	help	Hilfe		**scream**	Schrei
(to)	**hope**	hoffen	(to)	**smell**	riechen
	hope	Hoffnung		**smell**	Geruch
(to)	**interview**	interviewen	(to)	**taste**	schmecken
	interview	Interview		**taste**	Geschmack
(to)	**look**	aussehen	(to)	**work**	arbeiten
	look	Aussehen		**work**	Arbeit

Sioux pl. **Sioux** [su:, su:z]	Sioux-Indianer
frightening ['fraɪtnɪŋ]	furchterregend
gun [gʌn]	Schusswaffe
to **shoot, shot, shot** [ʃu:t, ʃɒt, ʃɒt]	schießen, schoss, geschossen
danger ['deɪndʒə]	Gefahr
on time [ɒn 'taɪm]	pünktlich

1 People

Fill in the right words (1–6) to find the missing word across (7).

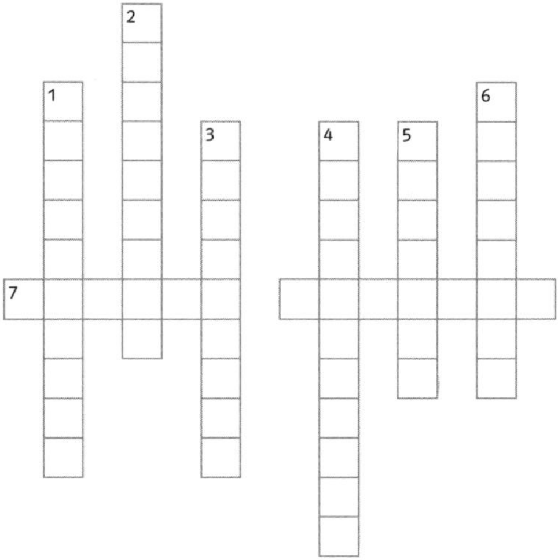

1. I help people and teach them about God.
2. I come when you call the ambulance.
3. I am on a journey.
4. People call me when there is a fire.
5. All the people in the world taken together are called …
6. My parents are King and Queen.

7. I am a ______________________________.

2 Word pairs

These word pairs sound almost or exactly the same. Use them to finish the sentences.

planned / plant   seat / sit   save / safe

whether / weather   write / right   gone / gun

bet / bed

1. Henry had ________________ to buy a new ________________ for his office.
2. The ________________ in this train are big enough for two, so ________________ down!
3. The ice on this lake doesn't look very ________________. I won't try ice-skating on it or you'll have to ________________ me!
4. The ________________ doesn't look very nice today. I'm not sure ________________ I should go hiking.
5. You'll never know what he thinks about you if you don't ________________ to him, ________________?
6. Did the burglar have a ________________? – Never mind, he's ________________ now.
7. Where is Martin today? – I ________________ he's still lying in ________________!

3 German and English words

Put in the English words. Underline the differences between the English and German words.

1. ______________________ = Nudel
2. ______________________ = Biografie
3. ______________________ = Komödie
4. ______________________ = Chemikalie
5. ______________________ = Prärie
6. ______________________ = (jemanden) warnen
7. ______________________ = fantastisch
8. ______________________ = Büffel

4 Wordsnake

All the adjectives and adverbs from Unit 6 are hidden in this wordsnake. Find them and write them down. Watch out! Sometimes it's more than one word.

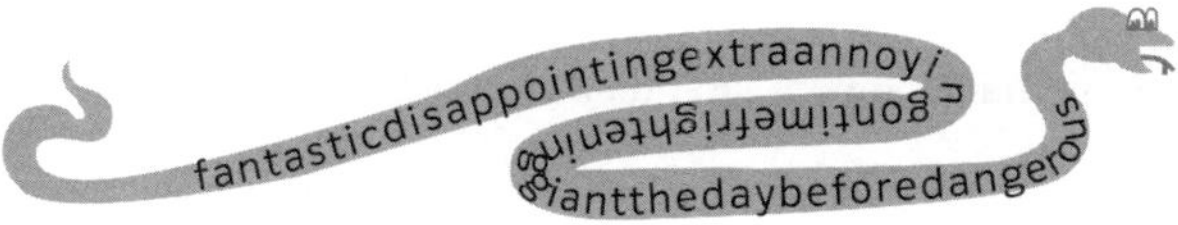

____

____

____

____

5 Definitions

Find the correct defintions of these words.

challenge | to introduce | to recommend | filler

whistle | bellow | delay | annoying

1. A high sound which is produced by your lips or an instrument: ________________
2. A loud angry shout: ________________
3. A difficult job you need lots of skills for: ________________
4. If a thing is … , it can make you angry. ________________
5. To tell someone that you liked something: ________________
6. An extra phrase you can use in a conversation: ________________
7. To start something new: ________________
8. Something happens later than planned: ________________

6 Verbs

Put in the correct verbs.

1. It ________________ 4 hours to get home by train!
2. Did he ________________ anything about the meeting?
3. The movie wasn't very exciting, we quickly

   ________________.
4. He ________________ us to go by train, not by car.
5. The doors didn't open, so we ________________ inside.
6. Did you manage to ________________ your report?
7. When we arrived in Glasgow, the train ________________.
8. After we had had a break, we ________________ on foot.
9. She suddenly ________________ loudly in the cinema!
10. The news ________________ that the burglar had

    ________________ 2 people. That's so horrible!

7 Phonetics

Write down the words.

1. [ˌiːvəˈluːʃn] ______________________
2. [pəˈsent] ______________________
3. [ˈwelkəm] ______________________
4. [ˈsɜːvɪs] ______________________
5. [ˈeəriə] ______________________
6. [huːz ˈɪn‿ɪt] ______________________
7. [suːz] ______________________
8. [ˈreɪlweɪ] ______________________

8 Hard or easy?

I thought these words in Unit 6 were …

easy	difficult

9 Words, words ...

Two words from every Unit in Green Line 3 are hidden in these boxes. Together with a partner try to find all of them. Who can find more? Compare your results.

B	O	B
S	L	E
H	G	I

____

A	C	S
T	I	T
H	L	E

____

O	T	C
R	V	I
I	A	N

____

L	L	E
E	W	R
J	E	Y

____

M	I	C
W	O	R
A	V	E

T	E	P
E	L	H
E	N	O

S	C	A
D	E	P
N	A	L

____

B	I	L
I	L	A
N	G	U

____

N	S	P
E	W	A
R	E	P

____

N	E	E
C	G	M
Y	R	E

____

R	E	T
L	L	R
E	V	A

____

L	L	A
E	E	H
N	G	C

____

10 The end and beginning

Find the letters the first word ends and the second begins with.

1. ov ___ ___ so
2. pit ___ ___ ance
3. swe ___ ___ hlete
4. ex ___ ___ ___ ion
5. empi ___ ___ ign
6. flo ___ ___ ganise
7. wi ___ ___ at
8. adv ___ ___ ___ hockey
9. diffi ___ ___ ___ ___ ure
10. leisu ___ ___ gion
11. ru ___ ___ cide
12. fir ___ ain
13. aweso ___ ___ dium
14. so ___ ___ plaud
15. ca ___ ___ age
16. whist ___ ___ ap
17. coa ___ ___ ange
18. ar ___ ___ gle

1 Round and round

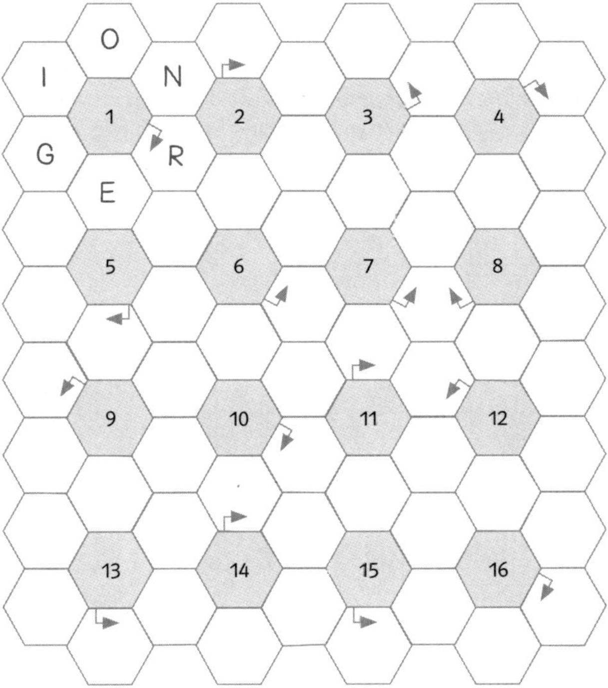

1. a part of a country
2. the opposite of old-fashioned
3. A spaghetti is a …
4. Sb from a foreign country speaks with an …
5. quiet
6. Concerts or festivals are …
7. We help our…
8. sth you don't want people to know
9. big towns
10. He works for the church.
11. Actors need it to rehearse their part.
12. There's no more … on my mobile.
13. You write a … to sb by post.
14. You can hit a ball with it.
15. sb who is crazy
16. The earth, sun or moon is a …

2 Battleships[1]

Play this game with a partner. Each of you writes 10 words from Green Line 3 into his/her field on the top. Now take turns to ask for the boxes in your partner's field on the bottom. If there is a letter in the box, your partner tells you and you note it down. You may ask again when you have hit a letter. The person who has found all his partner's words first is the winner!

	A	B	C	D	E	F	G	H	I	J	K	L	M	N
1														
2														
3														
4														
5														
6														
7														
8														
9														
10														

	A	B	C	D	E	F	G	H	I	J	K	L	M	N
1														
2														
3														
4														
5														
6														
7														
8														
9														
10														

[1]battleships [ˈbætl ʃɪps] – *Schiffe Versenken*

Lösungen

Unit 1

1 1 rugby 2 cricket 3 referee 4 track 5 court 6 athletics 7 umpire 8 racket

2 Down: 1 agreeing, 3 situation, 4 event, 6 place
Across: 2 rubbish, 5 definition, 7 race, 8 feeling

3 1 skateboarding 2 American football 3 sweat 4 eagle 5 gold medal 6 tradition 7 brake 8 to stop

4 helmet, pitch, base, field, bat, referee, oval

5 [əʊ] oval, snow, gold medal, rowing [ɒ] bobsleigh, oddity, goggles [ɔ:] record, skateboarding [ʌ] once, love

6 1 once 2 exact/exactly 3 also 4 far 5 might 6 not until

7 1 glasses 2 chances 3 halves 4 pitches 5 events 6 lungs

8 helmet, gold medal, van, glasses, wheelchair

9 1 controlling 2 sliding 3 flapping 4 waving 5 going on 6 opening 7 agreeing

10 baseball, cricket, athletics, rugby, skateboarding, ice hockey, American football, rowing, swimming, ski

11 Deine eigenen Antworten

Unit 2

1 Elizabethan, Protestant, Catholic, Victorian, Saxon, Norman, "I am a Briton."

2 1 Hi! 2 Bye! 3 See you later! 4 Hello!

3 steam engine, raw material, Industrial Revolution, middle name, European Union, connecting line, open day

4 steel, wood, power, stage, floor, free, gist, feed, shine, metal

5 to hate, to be connected, to joke, to reply, to clean, to drown, to continue, to nod, to keep out, to have no idea/ to wonder

6 1 fave 2 independent 3 modern 4 negative 5 odd 6 lonely 7 curious 8 close 9 old-fashioned

7 buildings: prison, tower, fortress; war: to attack, to defeat, knight; time: century, AD, age; people: poet, empress, heir, farmer

8 1a, 2b, 3b, 4b

9

T	A	C	T	U	A	L	L	Y	V
H	C	U	S	L	G	I	W	S	G
Y	T	E	S	X	F	N	Q	U	O
R	I	P	T	L	O	E	B	G	L
E	O	L	R	A	U	F	H	G	D
L	N	U	A	I	N	M	O	E	P
L	R	K	N	V	T	W	T	S	C
E	Z	C	G	H	A	A	R	T	V
W	E	I	E	Q	I	U	M	I	N
E	G	L	R	L	N	D	A	O	Y
J	D	C	F	C	L	E	A	N	O
P	I	N	V	E	N	T	I	O	N

10 1 wax 2 to gasp 3 servant 4 workshop 5 factory 6 telegram

11 Deine eigenen Antworten

12 Deine eigenen Antworten

Unit 3

1 (Lösungsvorschläge)
to get on: My sister and me get on very well.
to go out with: I'm going out with Jake tonight.
to turn into: My friend Thomas has turned into an idiot.
to get rid of: I had to get rid of my computer because I didn't have enough money.
to listen to: Listen to your mother when she gives you advice!
to tidy up: I tidied up my room yesterday.
to put on: My class is planning to put on a play.
to eat up: I don't want to eat up my dinner.

2 to meet, met, met; to split up, split up, split up; to stand, stood, stood; to feel, felt, felt; to leave, left, left; to grow, grew, grown; to eat up, ate up, eaten up; to get on, got on, got on

3 difference, especially, answerphone, secret, selfish, mind, advice, offer, jealous, grumpy

4

					1C					
2A	P	P	L	A	U	D				
					R					
3D	I	R	E	C	T	O	4R			
					A		E			5C
					I		H			O
6A	U	D	I	E	N	C	E			S
C							A			T
T					7L		R			U
R					I		S			M
E		8P	R	O	G	R	A	M	9M	E
S					H		L		A	
S					T				S	
	10P	R	O	P	S				K	

5 1. myself 2. yourself 3. himself 4. herself 5. itself 6. ourselves 7. yourselves 8. themselves

6 1. to marry 2. wise 3. bad luck 4. to tell a lie 5. not anymore 6. frozen 7. difficult

7 witch, telephone, mask, hat, twin(s)

8 1a 2b 3b 4a 5b 6a 7a 8b

9 1. Shut up! 2. You're driving me crazy! 3. Help yourself. 4. I see. 5. You've got a point. 6. Enjoy yourselves! 7. I'm afraid I can't come. 8. What's going on? 9. First things first. 10. I don't care.

10 1b 2a 3a 4b 5b 6a 7b

11 Deine eigenen Antworten

Unit 4

1 1 less 2 region 3 industry 4 Welsh 5 wing 6 taste 7 Asian 8 exhibition 9 dinner 10 audio

2 1 Sorry, I didn't mean to push you. 2 Take your time. 3 Never mind. 4 It's a pity. 5 I'd rather go home now.

3 to be into, to deal with, to get tired of, to make fun of, to try out, to hang out with

4 1 moved 2 deal with 3 exist 4 apologize 5 smell 6 seems 7 tastes 8 flows 9 cheered

5 1 on average 2 on the move 3 cult 4 article 5 relatives 6 firm 7 the poor 8 bilingual 9 birthplace

6 friendship, facelift, waterfront, heavy industry

7 1 recently 2 by 3 during 4 quite 5 at least

8 1 abstract, tea 2 curl, helping 3 reply, leisure 4 contrast, skim 5 culture, weird 6 topic, accent

9 1 keyword 2 coal mine 3 must-see 4 factual text 5 search engine

10 exchange, regional, engineer, awful, rude, curry, research, crowd

11 Deine eigenen Antworten

Unit 5

1 1 tube 2 bookworm 3 soap 4 newspaper 5 pile

2 1 copy 2 crack 3 allow 4 change 5 rewrite 6 organise 7 exchange

3 1 headline 2 the public 3 celebrity 4 couch potato 5 studio 6 LAN 7 advertisement 8 concert; The word is entertainment.

4 to attend a meeting, to reread a script, to discuss a topic, to create a new show, to cast a new star, to fall off a horse

5 an accident: ambulance, to tie, emergency, patient, blood, bandage, to rescue; a casting: to discover, agent, sides, to sign, file, contract, script

6 a) 1 noise 2 above 3 awesome 4 to photograph 5 to give your opinion

b) 1 passive 2 beginning 3 youth 4 to raise money 5 assistant

7 1 film 2 worth 3 disappear 4 admit 5 walk 6 cut 7 distract 8 attention

8 violence, outline, basic, argument, spinach, realistic, cold, product, roof, tight, housewife, soccer, cereal, violent, discussing, gash

T	F	B	S	P	I	N	A	C	H	V	L
N	O	V	D	U	R	H	P	W	Q	I	S
R	O	R	I	Y	C	O	Z	D	L	O	C
E	R	M	S	O	T	U	D	K	F	L	E
A	B	O	C	G	L	S	E	U	X	E	R
L	M	U	U	L	B	E	O	R	C	N	E
I	V	T	S	A	T	W	N	E	N	T	A
S	F	L	S	P	I	I	R	C	W	B	L
T	V	I	I	R	G	F	Q	C	E	S	D
I	C	N	N	O	H	E	M	O	L	I	C
C	P	E	G	A	T	G	H	S	A	G	H
U	A	R	G	U	M	E	N	T	Y	T	F

9 1 nickname 2 programme 3 look 4 magic 5 above

10 Deine eigenen Antworten

Unit 6

1 1 missionary 2 paramedic 3 traveller 4 firefighter 5 mankind 6 princess 7 police officer

2 1 planned/plant 2 seats/sit 3 safe/save 4 weather/whether 5 write/right 6 gun/gone 7 bet/bed

3 1 noodle 2 biography 3 comedy 4 chemical_ 5 prairie 6 to warn_ (sb) 7 fantastic 8 buffalo

4 fantastic, disappointing, extra, annoying, on time, frightening, giant, the day before, dangerous

5 1 whistle 2 bellow 3 challenge 4 annoying 5 to recommend 6 filler 7 to introduce 8 delay

6 1 took 2 mention 3 got bored 4 advised 5 were trapped 6 complete 7 slowed down 8 continued 9 screamed 10 reported/shot

7 1 evolution 2 per cent 3 welcome 4 service 5 area 6 Who's in it? 7 Sioux 8 railway

8 Deine eigenen Antworten

9 bobsleigh, athletics, Victorian, jewellery, microwave, telephone, landscape, bilingual, newspaper, emergency, traveller, challlenge

10 1 oval/also 2 pitch/chance 3 sweat/athlete 4 exact/action 5 empire/reign 6 floor/organise 7 wise/seat 8 advice/ice hockey 9 difficult/culture 10 leisure/region 11 rude/decide 12 firm/main 13 awesome/medium 14 soap/applaud 15 cast/stage 16 whistle/leap 17 coach/change 18 area/eagle

Puzzles

1 1 region 2 modern 3 noodle 4 accent 5 silent 6 events 7 selves 8 secret 9 cities 10 priest 11 script 12 credit 13 letter 14 racket 15 maniac 16 planet

2 Deine eigenen Antworten

List of irregular verbs

infinitive	simple past	past participle	German
to **be** [bi:]	**was / were** [wɒz, wɜ:]	**been** [bi:n]	sein
to **become** [bɪ'kʌm]	**became** [bɪ'keɪm]	**become** [bɪ'kʌm]	werden
to **bleed** [bli:d]	**bled** [bled]	**bled** [bled]	bluten
to **break** [breɪk]	**broke** [brəʊk]	**broken** ['brəʊkn]	(zer)brechen; kaputtmachen
to **bring** [brɪŋ]	**brought** [brɔ:t]	**brought** [brɔ:t]	(mit)bringen
to **build** [bɪld]	**built** [bɪlt]	**built** [bɪlt]	bauen
to **burn** [bɜ:n]	**burnt** [bɜ:nt]	**burnt** [bɜ:nt]	(ver)brennen
to **buy** [baɪ]	**bought** [bɔ:t]	**bought** [bɔ:t]	kaufen
to **catch** [kætʃ]	**caught** [kɔ:t]	**caught** [kɔ:t]	fangen
to **choose** [tʃu:z]	**chose** [tʃəʊz]	**chosen** ['tʃəʊzn]	(aus)wählen
to **come** [kʌm]	**came** [keɪm]	**come** [kʌm]	kommen
to **cost** [kɒst]	**cost** [kɒst]	**cost** [kɒst]	kosten
to **deal** (with) ['di:l wɪð]	**dealt** [delt]	**dealt** [delt]	(be)handeln
to **do** [du:]	**did** [dɪd]	**done** [dʌn]	machen, tun
to **draw** [drɔ:]	**drew** [dru:]	**drawn** [drɔ:n]	zeichnen
to **drink** [drɪŋk]	**drank** [dræŋk]	**drunk** [drʌŋk]	trinken
to **drive** [draɪv]	**drove** [drəʊv]	**driven** ['drɪvn]	fahren
to **eat** [i:t]	**ate** [et,eɪt]	**eaten** ['i:tn]	essen
to **fall** [fɔ:l]	**fell** [fel]	**fallen** ['fɔ:lən]	(herunter)fallen, hinfallen
to **feed** [fi:d]	**fed** [fed]	**fed** [fed]	füttern
to **feel** [fi:l]	**felt** [felt]	**felt** [felt]	(sich) fühlen
to **fight** [faɪt]	**fought** [fɔ:t]	**fought** [fɔ:t]	kämpfen; (sich) streiten
to **find** [faɪnd]	**found** [faʊnd]	**found** [faʊnd]	finden

infinitive	simple past	past participle	German
to **fly** [flaɪ]	**flew** [flu:]	**flown** [fləʊn]	fliegen
to **forget** [fə'get]	**forgot** [fə'gɒt]	**forgotten** [fə'gɒtn]	vergessen
to **get** [get]	**got** [gɒt]	**got** [gɒt]	holen, bringen; (be)kommen; werden
to **give** [gɪv]	**gave** [geɪv]	**given** ['gɪvn]	geben
to **go** [gəʊ]	**went** [went]	**gone** [gɒn]	gehen
to **grow** [grəʊ]	**grew** [gru:]	**grown** [grəʊn]	wachsen
to **hang** [hæŋ]	**hung** [hʌŋ]	**hung** [hʌŋ]	hängen
to **have** [hæv]	**had** [hæd]	**had** [hæd]	haben
to **hear** [hɪə]	**heard** [hɜ:d]	**heard** [hɜ:d]	hören
to **hide** [haɪd]	**hid** [hɪd]	**hidden** ['hɪdn]	(sich) verstecken
to **hit** [hɪt]	**hit** [hɪt]	**hit** [hɪt]	schlagen; treffen
to **hold** [həʊld]	**held** [held]	**held** [held]	halten
to **hurt** [hɜ:t]	**hurt** [hɜ:t]	**hurt** [hɜ:t]	verletzen, weh tun
to **keep** [ki:p]	**kept** [kept]	**kept** [kept]	behalten
to **know** [nəʊ]	**knew** [nju:]	**known** [nəʊn]	wissen; kennen
to **lay** [leɪ]	**laid** [leɪd]	**laid** [leɪd]	legen
to **learn** [lɜ:n]	**learnt** [lɜ:nt]	**learnt** [lɜ:nt]	lernen
to **leave** [li:v]	**left** [left]	**left** [left]	(ver)lassen; abfahren
to **lend** [lend]	**lent** [lent]	**lent** [lent]	leihen
to **let** [let]	**let** [let]	**let** [let]	lassen
to **lose** [lu:z]	**lost** [lɒst]	**lost** [lɒst]	verlieren
to **make** [meɪk]	**made** [meɪd]	**made** [meɪd]	machen, tun
to **mean** [mi:n]	**meant** [ment]	**meant** [ment]	bedeuten; meinen
to **meet** [mi:t]	**met** [met]	**met** [met]	(sich) treffen
to **pay** [peɪ]	**paid** [peɪd]	**paid** [peɪd]	(be)zahlen

infinitive	simple past	past participle	German
to **put** [pʊt]	**put** [pʊt]	**put** [pʊt]	setzen, stellen, legen
to **read** [ri:d]	**read** [red]	**read** [red]	lesen
to **ride** [raɪd]	**rode** [rəʊd]	**ridden** ['rɪdn]	fahren, reiten
to **ring** [rɪŋ]	**rang** [ræŋ]	**rung** [rʌŋ]	klingeln, läuten
to **run** [rʌn]	**ran** [ræn]	**run** [rʌn]	rennen, laufen
to **say** [seɪ]	**said** [sed]	**said** [sed]	sagen
to **see** [si:]	**saw** [sɔ:]	**seen** [si:n]	sehen
to **sell** [sel]	**sold** [səʊld]	**sold** [səʊld]	verkaufen
to **send** [send]	**sent** [sent]	**sent** [sent]	schicken
to **shake** [ʃeɪk]	**shook** [ʃʊk]	**shaken** ['ʃeɪkn]	schütteln
to **shine** [ʃaɪn]	**shone** [ʃɒn]	**shone** [ʃɒn]	scheinen; glänzen
to **shoot** [ʃu:t]	**shot** [ʃɒt]	**shot** [ʃɒt]	schießen
to **show** [ʃəʊ]	**showed** [ʃəʊd]	**shown** [ʃəʊn]	zeigen
to **sing** [sɪŋ]	**sang** [sæŋ]	**sung** [sʌŋ]	singen
to **sink** [sɪŋk]	**sank** [sæŋk]	**sunk** [sʌŋk]	sinken
to **sit** [sɪt]	**sat** [sæt]	**sat** [sæt]	sitzen
to **sleep** [sli:p]	**slept** [slept]	**slept** [slept]	schlafen
to **slide** [slaɪd]	**slid** [slɪd]	**slid** [slɪd]	rutschen, gleiten
to **smell** [smel]	**smelt** [smelt]	**smelt** [smelt]	riechen
to **speak** [spi:k]	**spoke** [spəʊk]	**spoken** ['spəʊkn]	sprechen
to **spend** [spend]	**spent** [spent]	**spent** [spent]	ausgeben; verbringen,
to **stand** [stænd]	**stood** [stʊd]	**stood** [stʊd]	stehen
to **steal** [sti:l]	**stole** [stəʊl]	**stolen** ['stəʊlən]	stehlen
to **swim** [swɪm]	**swam** [swæm]	**swum** [swʌm]	schwimmen
to **take** [teɪk]	**took** [tʊk]	**taken** ['teɪkn]	(mit)nehmen, bringen
to **teach** [ti:tʃ]	**taught** [tɔ:t]	**taught** [tɔ:t]	lehren
to **tell** [tel]	**told** [təʊld]	**told** [təʊld]	erzählen, sagen

infinitive	simple past	past participle	German
to **think** [θɪŋk]	**thought** [θɔːt]	**thought** [θɔːt]	denken, glauben
to **throw** [θrəʊ]	**threw** [θruː]	**thrown** [θrəʊn]	werfen
to **understand** [ˌʌndəˈstænd]	**understood** [ˌʌndəˈstʊd]	**understood** [ˌʌndəˈstʊd]	verstehen
to **wake** [weɪk]	**woke** [wəʊk]	**woken** [ˈwəʊkn]	(auf)wecken
to **wear** [weə]	**wore** [wɔː]	**worn** [wɔːn]	anhaben, tragen
to **win** [wɪn]	**won** [wʌn]	**won** [wʌn]	gewinnen, siegen
to **write** [raɪt]	**wrote** [rəʊt]	**written** [ˈrɪtn]	schreiben